MW00609213

Falling Through Time

A Collection of Poetry

By Sherry Lazarus Ross

WELL FIRE PUBLICATIONS
100 Markley St., Port Reading, New Jersey, 07064 USA

Well Fire Publications

FALLING THROUGH TIME
A Collection of Poems

Hardcover: 9780578996813

Published by Well Fire Publications
100 Markley St. Port Reading, NJ 07064

Cover & Interior Design by Platform House
www.platformhousepublishing.com

DEDICATION

In Memory of

Our son, Gregory Scott Ross

My parents, Leon Lazarus and Marjorie Olson Lazarus

My dear friend, Rickie Morrison

FALLING THROUGH TIME

Time is fluid.
Consciousness is
everywhere.
I am falling through time.
I can only trust
that like a common
sun transforming,
I will burn for a short space,
then become conscious.

FOREWARD

I had the pleasure of reading and reviewing Sherry Ross's first book of poetry, *Seeds of the Pomegranate*, so I already knew that immersing one's self in her poems would be like visiting a new country; one with unique sights to behold and adventures to be had. A foreigner to a new country will see things differently than natives and can offer insights un-thought of by the natives. The visitor, on the other hand, must often see or read something twice before they understand it. I for one really appreciate a place the second time I see it. So, it was when I read *Falling Through Time* twice, that the pages came alive to me with anticipation and I understood the genius of each poem and the poem maker.

A poem, like art, should always be judged by the sympathetic; for only they can have the 'seeing eye or ear.' As I read *Falling Through Time* I quickly cozied-up to the 59 poems arranged in three groupings – Relative Time (30), Story Time (14) and Cosmic Time (15). I had my favorites and you will too and they may not be the same. Most, wonderfully spoke to me, and some more than others. As with the best visual fine artists, it is often said, "only the mediocre are always at their best." I felt that the poems in this collection never fell below the excellent and at their best touched that place close to perfection. My staid crust was pierced again and again by Ross's penetrating insights, fresh turns of phrase, and blend of other-worldliness and common-place analogies. If art is condensed nature, then maybe poetry is condensed prose. Ms. Ross probes this very theme, the question of what is art and quality, in her poem "Optimism".

Sherry Ross is an authentic Gothic dream-landscapist, a nostalgic story-winder, a cosmic-conscious adept, and a faery conjuror. Certainly, she must be a 'sensitive' and a 'prescient' whose life is balanced between the rigors of a normal life and what seems, to this author's understanding, one also in touch with the 'twilight-world.' By this I mean the cosmos, faeries, gardens, fireflies, the dark wood, dusk, wetness after a rain or dew, slipperiness, moist dirt, autumn leaves, damp grass, remembrances, the lives of her family and herself – that mysterious Intersection with its very sheer veil. Scotland, as the capitol of the Elven kingdom, is a metaphor for much of her work.

Biographically she writes of her earliest sense of independence as an eight-year-old when she 'stole' "June's Red Bike." It was a confession of a victimless crime – joy riding at no one's expense, when she writes; *No one noticed I was late. No one saw my dirt and scrapes. No one ever asked about a missing bike. Not a thing was ever said, not a single repercussion came. With guilty heart, I'd performed the perfect crime.*

She writes in "A Poet's Work," *The trick is to catch a fish and not fall in. No, that's not it, the trick is to fall in and not drown, each time diving just a little further, so that I can bring back lost pearls, strange fossils, shimmering sea shells, bits of life, present and past: small treasures such as these.* That's what makes a true poet; the deeper they go, the deeper the poem.

Insight leaps from the second stanza of "All Grown Up", *As teens we gleaned that it was true that grown-ups didn't have a clue. We'd never make those sad mistakes, we'd surely know just what to do.*

Ms. Ross writes much like the painter, J-B Simeon Chardin paints his still-lifes, in her poem, "Each Day." *Each day for one week the pear stayed hard in the white china bowl. The other fruit we ate, the peaches and plums, softened, delicious and wanted, the apples and the bananas too. But no one ate the solid pear. It passed from forever seeming fresh into moldy rot before we knew, and so went untasted.*

In part two, <u>Story Time</u>, she writes in a Gothic voice in her brilliant, "The Faerie Encounter," in which a faery spurned a relationship, but scraped a mark, an Elven star, upon the chin of the poetess. It was a blessing and a curse, placing her between the human and the faerie worlds. She concludes, *And now until my days are truly done, I have no choice but wait to really know, by both great portals will I now be shunned? To which dear realm will then I finally go?*

In my opinion she saves the best for last when she leaps to <u>Cosmic Time</u> in part three. She waxes nostalgic and philosophical in poems, such as: "Cosmic Tour," *When I die I want the cosmic tour; to break gravity, pass GO and swing out into the stars, where galaxies scatter like so much salt on a hearty meal. I'll taste eternity, sip from time and feast till full.*

Questions, not over-burdened by answers, are contemplated in the third stanza of "The Dream Catcher's Song," *Is it calling me home with my own DNA? Has my number been dialed or can I still stay? Is it sending me elsewhere, a world dark and deep? Will I wake here on earth or die in my sleep?*

The last verse of "Ode to a Sunset" is particularly insightful. It is a poem about returning to our heavenly home: *The voyage back is eons long, each of us a different song. It's just a tale of getting home, by painful choices made alone.*

Our poetess sees that it is the simple things that really count "In All Directions" second verse, *How easy it is to slide into a larger object, one that seems grander, with more purpose and weight. But truly, when I do take the Big Slide, might I find that the greatest treasures are a cricket on the hearth, an autumn leaf hanging on a twig, the pattern on a moth's wings?*

She returns to family with her elegies, "Tell Me Who You Are: for My Father, Leon Lazarus" and "Grandpa Lazarus and the Light." Toward the end of her collection, in her short poem, "What is Possible?" we find an admission of truth and a higher reality: *I sense we are much more than what we think we are, but fall so short in this one small life.*

I want to read these poems yet again, but will wait until I can read them nicely published in book form. I am absolutely convinced that the third time will be the best.

Dr. Vern G. Swanson -

Dr. Swanson received his Doctorate from the Courtauld Institute of Art, University of London. He is the author and editor of over 20 books on Art, Culture and Religion, the author of such books as: *The Biography and Catalog Raisonne of the Paintings of Sir Lawrence Alma-Tadema, J.W. Godward 1861-1922: The Eclipse of Classicism, Dynasty of the Holy Grail, Soviet Impressionism,* and *Springville Museum of Art: History and Collection.* Dr. Swanson was the former Director of The Springville Museum of Art in Utah for 35 years and lectures internationally.

INTRODUCTION

Once upon a time there was a child and that child was me, or maybe it was you? Having entered my seventies, I have come to that moment in my own life where childhood, mine, often feels like a story from a larger tale, a legend of my own invention, a foreshadowing of the story of my life as it stands now. Time is strange, isn't it? That child we were, lived long ago, and yet there are moments when memories have collapsed, slid and bent in a way that makes older moments merge with the present. Sometimes an old memory feels fresher than a new one. We are the creators of our own story and in a way write and rewrite our lives, making a small legend of who we are. It is a way of processing our own identities and keeping ourselves intact. We are our own authors, taking even tragedy and loss and writing it into our personal legend to make it a whole, to try and make ourselves whole. We use our values, belief systems and experiences to write our tales and to keep ourselves integrated. I think that is why we love stories. We are always in one, editing and if need be, inventing just a bit.

That story is also all about time, something we can't define, but which rules us all our lives. In one way, time is merely a human construct that does not exist except as we have imagined it in order to function in our daily lives. It is also a reminder of our mortality. In another way, time is omnipresent, a super-reality, existing and permeating everything, always just beyond our human comprehension. It weaves in-between the vastness of space and in-between the vast spaces of our minds and it makes us a whole: the universe and each of us as individuals. Time encompasses everything, all of the past, present and future. Time, then, is truly timeless. This is not the kind of time we are familiar with in our daily lives, but something altogether different. For me, this other time has become synonymous with consciousness, the consciousness of this universe which holds in it all that has been, is and will be, with all the truths, laws and randomness that make it so. It is the great author, the teller of all stories and all histories simultaneously. It is the ultimate metaphor for reality in its fullest meaning. This all-encompassing reality shows us there is something bigger out there, wonderful, sometimes terrifying, but also miraculous and we are part of it. There is so much more than we can comprehend.

This collection of poems is a composite of a small amount of consciousness: mine. It is me falling through my time here on earth. The poems touch upon many emotions as well as philosophical and spiritual inquiries. I hope some of them will resonate with you and your own exquisitely unique and universal consciousness.

I have organized these poems into three sections, as different clusters of poems seemed to better represent different aspects of time. They are: Relative Time, Story Time and Cosmic Time. Relative Time is primarily autobiographical; my life as I remember it; as accurate as we are able to be. The poems in Story Time are either pure fiction or intentionally embellished autobiography. Cosmic Time holds my philosophical and spiritual beliefs. I have included some traditional forms of poetry, along with predominately contemporary free verse. You will find within these pages, free verse, rhyme, narrative poetry, sonnets and haiku.

TABLE OF CONTENTS

Part Two: Story Time

Part Three: Cosmic Time

RELATIVE
TIME

WE SEE WHAT WE WANT TO SEE

My feet scrunch on the wet lawn.
Clippings from the mowed grass stick to
my sneakers. Slugs are feeding on the
hostas mix in the shade at the edge of the garden.

Beetles cluster on the roses.
The ground writhes with life.
We see what we want to see and
sometimes what we don't.

Eyes are everywhere, objective and
single-minded. Now the sound of rain
overwhelms the noise of chewing.
I will not resort to poison.

Ferns and pink astilbe make love
under the ivy, which winds around a
piece of driftwood we placed here years ago,
a green patina spreading across its silver surface.

I enter the far gate onto a carpet of moss.
I imagine the splash of water – a fountain
with shallow pool and bronzed satyr
holding court. It is all so real, this mirage.

Everything changes and yet remains the same.
A vision of what has been and what will come.
A vision of what is now and what will never be.
A time to pinch off dead azalea blooms.

A DREAM BEFORE THE BIRTH OF OUR DAUGHTER

I stand on a raft of bark and twine.
Around me the lake is calm glass.
It is neither day nor night.
Moonlit fish swim toward me.
They are white and round,
glowing orbs that propel
themselves out of the water onto the
raft at my feet, weak and helpless as
the unborn.
I feel lost.
There is a cry from the woods.
It is the she wolf's mate. I look.
My husband stands on the
edge of the lake and calls to me.
His mouth moves, "Come, come,"
but there is no sound. His hand beckons.
I slide into the water, warm and shallow.
My belly rides the sand ploughing forward
until I stop – small stones in my mouth.
Quickly I lift on all fours and climb to land,
my mate ahead of me in the forest.
Now my feet are wearing hiking boots.
There are provisions to be had.
On a branch I find a pitcher of milk and a
willow basket filled with small loaves of bread.
The forest fades and I am in a grocery store.
I push a large cart in front of me,
brimming with necessities.
Outside the cars and houses are not familiar.
It is rural here.
I carry my package into the dark.

My boots work hard up a hill,
a narrow path on the edge of town.
My family, where will I find them?
I remember: in the family room, the den.
It begins to rain.
A breeze stirs and I smell the lake.
I like the way the earth
moves spongy under my feet.
I like the close smell of
fertile earth.
Something moves.
I feel the ground tremble.
Soon, it will happen soon.

While Working in the Garden

Come here and I will show you
something not quite born.
The size of an unshelled pecan,
it is lollipop green with a
yellow tipped "tail" like a young
evergreen branch in spring.
Look, its lids are still sealed.
What eyes would they reveal?
You frighten me, unknown organism.
What is my connectedness to you?
I feel like kicking you under last year's
nettle behind the holly bush.
But that won't do.
I have seen your strangeness,
alien embryo, the size of a peanut.
I won't forget you.
I could squash you in an instant
but my murderous thoughts hold me back.
Who are you, forgotten foundling;
a stunted fetus, a misplaced soul,
a trust, broken?
I suppose it's your vulnerability that so
unnerves me.
You are so marsupial,
premature, a damaged beginning
torn from your mother's sack.
I would like to forget I've seen you.
But I can't.
With a stick I roll you under the
beech tree's roots, out of sight.

THE OLD APARTMENT
FOR MY GRANDMA, RACHEL LAZARUS

The apartment house is still here.
How can that be?
It was torn down thirty years ago.
I step into the entrance hall,
cross over the art deco floor,
brittle octagon tiles, black
and cream like old bones,
grout brown with dirt and age and
press the button of the lift.
The dim light in the round window
brightens as it grinds to a halt.
The door opens.
I enter and hit number three,
the magical number of
timeless tales, and rise.
It comes to a stop.
There, in front of me,
her door is ajar,
She is waiting.
"Grandma!
How can you be alive?"
So thin, a skeleton really,
I fold her in my arms, telling her:
"I miss you so."

FEAR OF THE DARK

The sound of my father's typewriter
is pop-corn popping at a great speed.
It is a lullaby — one of my first sounds.
My mother sings softly during the day
so she won't disturb my father's work.
I am a special child with two lullabies.
In the night, unwanted in my blue cage,
I hear another song not meant for me.
The sounds and shadows are frightening.
It is here I learned to fear the dark.

Eleven Months Old

I pull myself from the
boundaries of my crib onto the
windowsill, the top of the dropped
bars are level with the sill and
the waiting city street.
Ground level, the window
opens to the spring air,
has yet more bars,
more signs of captivity.
I crawl, turn and push
my head through a very tight
space, overcoming two
attempts at imprisonment.
With a twist of my shoulders
I birth myself out onto the
rough wet sidewalk.
I feel the grit of the
tiny pebbles against my
baby palms.
Such adventure,
crawling down the street.
There is a shout and then
Mama scoops me in her arms.
Oh, the disappointment.

JUNE'S RED BIKE,
EIGHT YEARS OLD

The first time I felt independent
was on June's red bike.
A summer evening,
dinner done, fireflies blinking
in the shadows of the bushes,
sky still lit with electric pink and
lavender at the horizon; I knew
I had another twenty minutes before
the call to bath and bed.

I was alone, no friends shouting
or running about. It was quite unusual.
So I slipped around the corner and
there against the apartment's
brick wall it rested, shiny, bright,
beautiful, but just a bit too small,
with training wheels still on.
Surely she wouldn't mind a spin?
After all, I wasn't stealing it.

My leg flew over and I was on the
seat. I struck that kick stand and
up and off I went, flying down the
alley between buildings, out onto the
sidewalk, my feet kept dragging on the
ground; a right onto Bruce Street,
I headed toward Shaler Boulevard.
So free. Why, I bet I could ride
all the way to New York City.

I soared by houses I'd passed slowly on
foot each day to school. The air against my
skin wonderful, the smell of honeysuckle
delicious, the sky darkening, becoming a
world not meant for children - so thrilling.
Sound was altered. Cars, come home late,
seemed muffled, more poetic, and voices
mysterious, distant and dreamlike.

What were other families like?
Were they happier, sadder, richer,
did they watch the same TV shows?
I coasted down the hill and over the
footbridge in a streak of speed and joy.

At the corner, where the stores began,
I knew it was time to turn around. The shops
had closed, the street was empty.
It was the quietest of moments.

I stopped and sat, looking down the
street, then up into the twilight sky.
Time stood still and it seemed I had
forever in my range of vision - forever to
do what I would do, to be what I would be.
Such layers of inexplicable aching beauty.
A car passed; the enchantment was broken.
A dog barked. I smelled roasting coffee.
It was time to head back home.

I was sailing up the incline, back over the
footbridge when it happened. The handle
bars shimmied, jiggled, jerked and came
right off the bike. I toppled to the side,
dirty and bruised, but not much hurt.
Too big for June's bike, just as Goldilocks,
I had broken it. With stealth I slid first the bars,
then bike, down the embankment under the
bridge and out of sight. I walked back home.

No one noticed I was late. No one saw my
dirt and scrapes. No one ever asked
about a missing bike. Not a thing was
ever said, not a single repercussion came.
With guilty heart,
I'd performed the perfect crime.

THE ACCIDENT

Wheels skid on road top.
Flung up-side-down the
earth falls away.
Here is the abyss, the
awaited transition.
Terror grips and then
mercy peels off the sharp
edge of pain
slaying the first death —
leaving, clear, two bright
red tears where wings
will surely grow.

FRIENDSHIP AT FOURTEEN

Early Saturday mornings
we would meet lean and
hungry with no breakfast,
booted with striped scarves
untied, hanging round our necks
like misplaced prayer shawls.
We walked for hours,
especially through graveyards,
read the stones and
told stories to each other,
laughed, never paid attention
to the cold or other people,
only to the moment.
We walked and walked, with
nothing but the future
straight ahead.

A Poet's Work

I feel myself fall
against the flesh of being.
I try to gather the very
air into my arms.
I live far into joy, on
its edge, just where it
begins to sting.
It seems my eyes
dilate too freely.
They let too much inside.
I've become accustomed to a
new metabolism,
one that burns air,
time, ash and woody
mushrooms. True,
sometimes I'm agitated,
but I can check that now,
the untethered churning of
stardust and waterfalls.

Some people go
scuba-diving on holiday.
I go fishing every day
in odd places.
The trick is to catch
a fish and not fall in.
No, that's not it,
the trick is to
fall in and not drown,
each time diving
just a little further,

so that I can bring back
lost pearls, strange fossils,
shimmering sea shells,
bits of life, present and past:
small treasures such as these.

THE FREELANCE WRITER
MEMORIES BEFORE THE DIGITAL AGE

The rhythm of her day
is tied to the postal hour.
The weeks pass and she forgets
each morning
that she is waiting.
There is work to do and she
is by now disciplined.

The ache begins as afternoon
approaches – the hour of delivery.
Despite her willfulness
her heart quickens in
anticipation. Yes, she is
waiting for reassurance, one
that never comes, like a pen-pal
lost in childhood, a friendship
through the mail
never fully realized.
But today could be the day.
The day of confirmation.

Or will they all return:
poems, stories, novels, essays –
rejected one and all –
each a mutilated stillborn?

What kind of life is this?
No matter how many hard won
victories, always this dull
ache in the afternoon,
this moment of thrill and loss
like clockwork, this
brutal passivity.
She must do something.
Do something.
But what?
In the morning,
she will write.

SORROW

The SOR's for the
sore – the hurt – the
O for the shape
your mouth makes
in pain –
the OW for the sound
that comes from
your mouth.
The SORR
for sorry –
guilt and shame –
the ORROW
an arrow
shot through your heart.

BITTER

Bitter – the flavor
permeates the mouth,
affects all taste –
even the sweetest sweet
turns bitter sweet.

Live on one food only
and you'll grow ill,
unbalanced and oddly
damaged over the
long haul.

You can't live life
by a single strategy or
expect one definitive to
answer all your needs –
life fights rigidity.

Existence is fluid,
multi-dimensional and
unstoppable - has no patience for
your anger and angst and will
pass you by, leaving you bitter.

OPTIMISM

It is said that people
no longer recognize quality,
are deadened on junk
food and junk culture.
But if that is true
why are craft shows
packed to brimming –
hundreds holding pottery,
turning pieces
in their hands
to check for evenness and form?
And the poetry festivals?
Damn, you need a
shuttlebus just to get in –
so much enthusiasm.
Why does everyone I speak to,
the butcher, the baker,
beautician, teacher, painter,
all complain of shallow TV shows,
then recommend those with great acting,
meaningful themes and excellent
character development?

Who am I kidding?
There are mountains of junk out there.
Whole new geographies of it
growing every day.
But here we all are,
small gods on the dump heap –
picking, choosing, sorting through.
We're not dead. We're hungry.

First Fall

A spotted orange leaf,
avant-garde and witty,
flew itself, stem first,
through the open
summer window and
landed atop my dormant
pen.

Here we go after
a slow season - straight
to excitement.

It's good to feel this rush of
coming change; an unexpected
gift placed upon my desk, startling
me, pleasantly, into consciousness.
In the fall, time is like an
orange-spotted leaf,
wild and unpredictable.

All Grown Up
For My Granddaughters Kayleigh and Anna

As children we would play all day
pretending we had full control,
so free to do as we might please,
with meals of ice cream in a bowl.

As teens we gleaned that it was true
that grown-ups didn't have a clue.
We'd never make those sad mistakes.
We'd surely know just what to do.

As grown-ups, work and taking roles
took up the minutes of our days.
It gave us skills but took its toll,
we longed for days in which to play.

And now I'm old and turning grey,
my grandkids hide, command and play
while I cajole and act the fool
to keep them laughing after school.

DAILY CYCLES
THREE HAIKU FOR RELATIVE TIME

Lamplight on the sheets,
patterns of dreams and deep sleep
broken by the sun.

The smell of morning,
coffee and honeysuckle,
salt air and seaweed.

The shimmer of sea,
Sands, sprinkled with towels and pails,
children's voices sing.

TREASURE

One handful of
chipped seashells
glint brightly, like
miniscule rainbows.
Lilliputian rafts of
splintered light
travel along the angled
channels of my palm.
To be so small,
to be so radiant,
to think I almost
didn't notice.

BOYS

The cold wave breaks
against the lean
bone and muscle of
their perfect boy-ness.
Four distinct shrieks,
breaths sucked in,
the ribs out,
identical taut stomachs,
arms flying, hands punching,
protecting and inviting.
They had to be here,
the black rocks, the whelks
and glistening seaweed,
the cold waves breaking -
demanded it.

EACH DAY

Each day for one week
the pear stayed hard in the
white china bowl.
The other fruit we ate –
the peaches and plums softened,
delicious and wanted,
the apples and bananas too.
But no one ate the solid pear.
It passed from forever
seeming fresh into moldy rot
before we knew, and so
went untasted.

GRANDPA'S PRAYER
FOR JACOB LAZARUS

Grandpa
peels an orange with
due reverence.
Skillfully
he works his knife and
with it draws a
perfect strip of
sunshine into the air –
one continuous ribbon of
rind and pulp.
The familiar smell
brings with it waves and
palm trees, billowing sails
headed for adventure,
all the stories
we have ever shared.
Not a word is said.
His two thumbs
split the fruit in half –
I reach for mine.

La Toilette
For Fred

Helen of Troy
styled her hair and
Nefertiti too – as
here before my mirror
I do my hair for you.

This simple act,
now made complex, is
fraught with contradictions.
But as I do my hair for you,
it's merely sweet affection.

A Gardener in Her Garden

In the rain the garden grows
a deeper green – the leaves varnished,
shining, primroses phosphorescent in
pinks and reds and an orange that startles.
I imagine a stone path running back
toward the woods to a gentle flowing fountain,
the gurgle and the sunlight catching something
glinting and living in the water.
This is next year's project, perhaps? The
imagining of a garden is as rich as any tale.
The allium are late and rise monstrous
out of the border like giant dandelion puffs
gone haywire and purple with mutation.
I've always felt a garden should disturb
us just a bit – a dense peacefulness with
unexpected shocks of shape and color
around the bend, surprises, pleasant but
unnerving, safe, but full of potent magic.

GLASS DARKLY

I catch the doe out of the
corner of my eye and see
her clearer now than
yesterday, when she stood
before me, then fled in fear.

Sometimes, to see
indirectly, is the clearest
way to see, more authentic,
a vivid glimpse through
the glass darkly.

CARROT UNICORN
FOR KARA

I turn the corner from
the kitchen to the den,
bearing a gigantic carrot
pressed against my head.
Stepping out into view I
wear a bright vegetable horn.

My daughter, then six, shrieks
with glee and disbelief.
Her mom turned unicorn
before her eyes, still loving but
altered and surreal. "It's the
largest veggie in the world!"

Later, at dinner time,
when I place the bowl of
buttered orange discs
gently on the table, my daughter
bows with dignity and states:
"All from just one carrot!"

FOR MY DAUGHTER KARA
NOW A MOM

Your sweet child's face
floats before me as an
apparition that fades in and
out, accompanying me through
all my daily chores.

I place the towels in the linen-
closet and look across the
upstairs hall, through the opened
door and into your old room, the
same, but now perpetually neat.

There you are, legs crossed
sitting on your bed in a deep place,
bits of paper scattered on the
bedspread, strings with beads, lanyards;
you turn and look right through me.

Grown now, I love you dearly,
but this other face, eyes asking,
wanting, searching, becoming –
is gone forever and she haunts me.
Sweetly haunts me still.

For Gregory
An Early Memory of My Son

I should have known
you'd be a poet.
At eighteen months
you pointed to an autumn leaf –
blazing red – and
proclaimed with great intensity:
"Fire!"
I thought you meant it
literally, and were alarmed.
So I told you soothingly,
reassuringly,
"It's just a leaf,
just a leaf changed color."
You burst into tears,
indignant, insistent,
"No! Fire, fire!" you shouted and
plucked it fearlessly from the pile.
My lights went on,
"You mean it looks like fire!"
It was your first metaphor and
you broke into the biggest smile.
I should have known
you'd be a poet and like
that blazing leaf and
poetry itself, your life
intense and short.

For My Uncle, Sidney Lazarus
Artist, Poet and Mentor

This Poem Was Inspired By His Visual World of Art

He built watchful firefly midnights with
still inhabitants who waited for Juicy Morning,
with her picnic basket and boysenberry breasts,
to whip up a batch of crabgrass pancakes and
scrambled moss, over lightly, with cups of violet tea.

He talked to me of Poe and James and
anti-social Emerson, then pulled out charts and
maps till weary-eyed we'd laugh and take a
break at midnight to eat chunks of marble
halvah and drink strong black Turkish coffee.
He'd say, "Let's see who can be the least profound,
the most absurd," and giggled in his cup.

He dreamt and blue ink became pale lace and
odd numbers, one through nine, with arms and legs,
marched up the infinite edge of fresh paper onto Jupiter:
bottles spilling drunken genies, monstrous cakes eating
drunken men, Bacchus drinking Welch's grape juice and
pinching the plump ass of a willing, laughing damsel.

His eyes then moved somewhere else,
upstate New York in August with all of us
out on the screened porch, smelling the apple orchard,
talking about self-actualization, eating Aunt Sylvia's
home- baked cornbread, the rabbi arguing with Dad,
Dad arguing with Sid and Harry, Sid arguing with
everyone and no one taking any of it too seriously.

He fantasized with colored pencils and
Lady Whimsy came to life, an Elven Queen who
grew wild-eyed carrots in her earthen pots,
lustful Ids with curly tops, coveting the too ripe
contents of the gold fruit bowl, with its grapes slipping
off their skin tight clothes, sweet peach juice
collecting on the table, an old ant, sketched in
black, thinking he found Paradise.
I'd say, "My, that's good."
He'd say, with pencil lifted,
"It's only hand-fruit, don't you see?
It grows from out my fingertips."

When he schemed, night pulled back
over a bright kettle of green pea soup,
white steam pouring into the cold air,
three demons whooping it up under an
old lantern, hung up in an old tree,
crumbling their stale bread into their clay
mugs, slapping their sharp knees, mumbling
their Fae spells into the late night.
He'd say,
"Who said
winter's hues
are drab and lifeless?
Look at all these
browns and browns."

He built deep blue ceilings into the secure
womb of the sinking sun, where watchful fireflies
worshipped the endless energy of the endless June
bugs and secret planets sang to the open meadows and

the August heat, with its smell of apples, the juice dripping
on the summer table.
He'd say,
"The pain is less."
I'd say,
"You look so tired."
God I miss him.

SISTERS
FOR MY SISTER ROCHELLE LAZARUS SAXENA

We have collected our losses.
Between us quite a few by now.
How much we share. Not only
in taste and passions, so similar
we often buy the same gifts,
unknowingly, but also in memories;
that internal understanding of the
substrata that makes up our histories,
our motivations, weaknesses
as well as strengths, remarkably
similar. This sisterhood we share
is rich, deep, and grows ever more
enduring.

Years older than you,
there was a time I felt almost like
your mother; even when our mom
was here. But as the years have passed,
you have come to mother me as much
as I can mother you.
We are peers, best friends, and
gratefully, sisters.

WE LIVED:
IN MEMORY OF MY MOTHER MARJORIE OLSON LAZARUS

LAKE MICHIGAN

You lived and all your years before me are mine too.
Always, through both our lives, there is The Lake;
its waves breaking madly against the lighthouse,
drumming the stone walkway wet and slippery, ready
to cast us over the edge into the churning, pounding
body of fresh water, a lake big enough to challenge the
sea when she is wild and in the throes of unleashed weather.

The swells hit the walkway and soak us through. When
young I made those windy, wet walks too.
Exciting, triumphant, I relish imagining your youthful
balance, reckless, agile steps and compare them to my own,
now, too, only a memory.

THE HOUSE

Here, right now, we are at the old house, the house built
by your father. Grandpa's hands planned the plumbing,
ran the wire and tilled the garden out back. You picked
strawberries and rhubarb here, with Grandma, for her famous
rhubarb pie. So did I. In late August the concord grapes
grew fat and ready for dark rich jam and family wine. I stole
a sip at nine. Let us walk through this old house together,
count the corners, touch the doorways, smell the musk of the
attic's past, with its one dark terror held still as death -
a cold spot that's left its chill, marking a time of less laughter,
when your sister became ill - secrets that haunted your childhood,
then mine.

The Cellar

Floating fast away from here, like Alice down the rabbit
hole, we descend the cellar staircase, pass the storage pantry,
a scattering of old canned goods, poison by now, and take the
second set of smaller stairs.

Arrived, we find, lying drowsy under sawdust, all the
useful utensils of invention, hanging from the walls, fast asleep.
How busy all these tools once were, the lath and chisel,
hammer and pinch-nosed-pliers, the little cans of useful
screws and sturdy nails, now rusted red with the moon's
wet cycles.

Look, stacked along this first shelf, Grandpa's countless
notebooks, brimming with mechanical drawings and detailed
tests of trial and error, ideas that took hold and thrived, vibrated
inside with that gleam of something newly born from out the
mind, that lives and shines.

Hollywood and Myth

Later, you pulled out scrapbooks from your teens,
as many as your father's, with pictures coming loose,
headlines sizzling and presented me with the
Golden Age of Hollywood.

You made it dance and sing through daytime
reveries, in talk and old-reruns; mine a phantom version
in black and white, but still elegant and influential,
yours the culmination of glamor and glitz and life lived
right, electric with excitement, love and sin.

Oh, you so loved the gossip of the stars,
sharing the heartache of Nelson Eddie and
Jeanette MacDonald, bringing pathos and
drama onto the internal stage of my imagination.
Fairytales, myths and legends, all those too
passed to me through you.

THE BEDROOM

Now let us climb back up the stairs, gingerly
pass the hall window, with its fluttering, gauzy
drapery, like flimsy shrouds, floating outward in
the night's breeze to brush us with paranormal
leanings and maybe even evil itself.

These are the bedrooms, the beds, closer to
the wind's thick world of puzzling travel,
the attic above haunts and groans with age.

We imagine drinking dreams at the windowpanes,
the clear thin stream of liquid glass, awash with
breathy gusts, gushing currents, broken signs and
symbols, rushing us off to some exotic land, hypnotized
with the mirage of our futures.
We both had dreams in this room,
here, tucked into our ancestral beds.   —

In these sheets thin and frayed, I watched
all night the shifting blue of the gathered closet
curtains. They moved like rippling waves, from
the lake, coming ever closer, reaching for my
outstretched toes until the morning whistle and
rumble of the passing train brought comfort.

This was your room, your waves, your morning train.
Do you remember? Hidden behind the watery drapes
we found your beloved doll, Rosie, in pale pink, her
composition arms and legs cracked, but her face
still sweet and in that moment, I adopted her

TEATIME AND HOLIDAY

Who will love our dolls now; now when we are
gone? We both made worlds of miniatures, dressing
still babies in beautiful blue brocade, setting them up to
have tea in the dining room, or opening tiny presents
by a doll size tree, glittering with holiday anticipation.
It was in the old dining room that your childhood tree
stood, here, by the Victorian breakfront, a Hans Christian
Anderson work of glory, with clip-on candles, no longer
used, too dangerous, but seen by you lit once or twice
when you were a child.

Later, when you became a mom, our tree was much smaller,
but adorned with all your sparkling creations, a splendid time,
when melancholy lifted off of you and wonder ruled our home –
till bleak January arrived - my birth month.

THE PORCH

Let's leave the dining room slowly, with some grace, and
turn onto the summer porch, enclosed, since 1948, with
stacks of books, cozy chairs, chintz and checkered,
wicker and wood. The warm rain, gentle, is always soothing -
a peach in hand, a fuzzy kiss, then splendid juiciness and the
smell of heaven.

Looking up I see the large black rings from which you said once hung a sliding swing for two. I touch the air and feel it glide and move.

THE ARRIVALS

One June, when I was eight, a baby girl arrived,
the center of your world it seemed… my sister.
Grandma came to help for four months.

Sequestered you slept and fed and grandma ruled,
cooking all the dishes that belonged in Michigan,
not here in our kitchen. Nothing tasting quite right.
Me, cast to the side, the childhood drama of
"no one loves me anymore."
Talks with dad didn't help,
too cerebral for this much emotion, and he too
focused on you and the new life.

But then, in time, I learned what a blessing really means, for,
sweet sister, we share these same old ghosts and dreams.

GRANDMA'S KITCHEN

And how we do remember Grandma's kitchen, where she was
meant to cook! It was stupendous, an event, a culinary coup of
comfort food, so many up-side-down galettes were baked,
pineapple and brown sugar turning caramel, short cake and
strawberries, potatoes and heavy cream both beaten into thick
perfection with just one hand spinning like a top, the other
holding the bowl in place against her chest, snug and firm,
making alchemy, edible magic. We, all three, watched her
conjuring while growing up.

FINALE

No more kitchen noise, oven heat or wooden spoons stirring.
No more smells of ginger, nutmeg and cinnamon, or
while dinner simmered, the happy play at the piano.
Grandpa on the violin, taught himself at seventy and lived
till 94. No more.

The keys chipped and tuneless, the piano long gone.
There still rings out fading, vibrating echoes, that sing,
"There lingers, there will always linger."

So Mom, let us walk this house one final time
before these walls come down, are torn apart and
newer things are made. You know I understand.
I understand it well:
They lived, then they lived,
we lived, then they lived.

STORY TIME

A HAUNTING AT....
CRAIGIEVAR CASTLE, SCOTLAND

A tourist says to her husband:

"There was so much love here.
Remember how we ran along
this deep green furrow of earth,
overgrown with moss and fern,
that drops below the roadway?

Remember my mama and papa, so long
ago? They, home in the family carriage
from a week's stay at Aunt Laetitia's,
the hooves and wheels passing us by,
we, hidden in the green ditch?

You were my first love, my
first kiss at fourteen.
They say you must acquire
a taste for kissing, but your mouth
was made for mine, it needed no acquiring.

Then, when my baby brother died,
found dead in the cradle,
Mama went silent and
Papa went away on business.
You held me like glue, together.

I don't remember more...

That is why it startles me now,
how can you not understand
when I tell you it's all the same,

the road, the ditch, the house,
the windows."

The husband, while scrolling his iPhone:

"But Honey, we've only
toured here once before,
five years ago. You said the
same odd thing back then."

THE WOLF BOY
A TERRIBLE NIGHTMARE OF INFANTICIDE

My boy came to me last night
out of the wet leaves with the
head of a wolf in his arms.
He stroked its matted hair and
kissed its bruised cheeks.
I screamed on the top of my voice,
"Drop that filthy thing!"
He grinned wolfishly, willfully, and
shoving his fist into the mangled neck
shook the horrid thing at me
like a puppet on a stick and
stepped towards me
out of the woods.

I turned and ran to the house
but by some dark magic
everything had changed.
The doors wouldn't bolt,
the windows were jammed open,
the sinks were filled with sewage,
the toilet kept flushing itself.
I was trapped –
a doomed rabbit in its broken hutch.
My boy had changed, become the wolf.
I grabbed a baseball bat and blindly
beat and beat.

SCORPIONS

I arrive home, but
now our room is chalk white and
I've entered from a long white hall.
She sits on your lap smiling, this stranger.
It's a perfect portrait,
your faces whiter than the white walls,
eyes glazed, teeth, too long,
showing within your smiles.

Something moves nearby -
little hot lies, red fire on tiny legs
they dart, move down the drapes,
spread across the sheets,
bright pain spots on the stark
blank whiteness.
There is a thud on the rug next to me.
The scorpions have emerged.

SCOTLAND: LOVE STILL LINGERING
A SONG

I know I've stood here
once before as
clouds swept past
these purple hills;
it was a time, a time before,
I still belonged to
others' wills.

A drawing back,
I feel its strength,
it pulls me taut– an arrow
in its bow –
it draws me back, an
arrow in its bow -
I hold and then let go.

I know I've walked
these paths before and
rested by these trees.
The day seems warm
but nights, I warn,
grow harsh and cold, don't
lose your way and freeze.

I remember now from
where I came and everything
is just the same,

so, I'll lay down and
wait my claim while,
listening sweetly with
no blame.

I know just where to
go and nest and
wait the bitter through –
to wait the bitter through,
I know just what to do.
I'll come straight
back to you.

A drawing back,
I feel its strength,
it pulls me taut – an arrow
in its bow –
it draws me back – my
aim is you –
you hold me, then let go.

POSSESSED

I have seen you.
You were in the house
of my mother and father
all those years ago, weren't you?
Then came the golden light.
Bathed in it I was blinded and
forgot you. But you were there -
the great matter of things
left behind.

Then began the long
gazing in the mirror,
the hypnotic longing
catching in our eyes:
"Sometimes in the glass I see
someone I'm surprised to be."
How beautiful we are,
each like a lover looking at
his new love, or then our faces
twisted in an odd way,
the mouths all wrong.

But last night
my conscious mind
opened in my dream
and I beheld you,
strange being the color of rock,
a wide and hungry look.
I was wary,

suspicious, but not fear-struck.
Our eyes met and I could see
you too were wary of me.
What human eyes you had.

Now, locked in a
practiced dance
we circle, move quickly,
me over you, you over me —
then, with a sure-footed step
to the side, I understand:
the light makes shadow.

A RETURNING

Displaced, hungry,
it is hard to return to a
world we can't quite remember —
a strange dimension of
folded foliage pulled green
over a hidden seed.

The glass clear river
has banks edged deep,
slices of earth cake
made for a mountain lord
of clean dark dirt
frosted with moss.

The soft hills surround.
It is a rocking in the cradle,
the quiet before waking,
the sleep that is a
waking sleep,
not a dream.

We have been here before.
The sun rains light and
the rain is a sadness
washed away —
blissful,
blank.

Twilight and dawn
will raise us off our knees —
the terrible
the wonderful
fused this instant
into harmony.

BRUEGELESQUE: LAST AUTUMN RITUAL

Twelve men hoist the nearly
two-thousand-pound pumpkin
onto the sturdy wagon – making
it the Heart of Harvest on display.
Below, earth's chest reveals a
dented, shallow wound, where veins
and vines still cling to the mother
skin of rich brown dirt.

The largest vein, from which the stem
is now detached, pulses with a deepening
greenish-purple hue and is both aorta and
umbilical to the giant orange organ, its
source and flow of nutrients and photosynthesis.

To the left, men and women dig a trench.
To the right, others gather branches,
twigs and leaves, needed for the ritual pyre.

Will the heart of harvest be returned to its
weighted earthly body or sacrificed to an autumnal blaze,
its seeds crackling and bursting beyond fertility?

One among them steps
forward and with an ax cleaves
out a wedge of rind and meat.
A massive bowl appears,
flashes silver in the twilight.

The chosen one sinks hands
into the soft, pulpy flesh, and
scooping forward fills the vessel
full of juice and white glistening seeds.

The sun sets.
The fire burns.
There is music,
merriment,
dancing.

PHILOSOPHICAL OWL IN THE APPLE ORCHARD

Looking down I
see the apple orchard —
the twisted branches are
reassuring wombs,
lovely limbs of shelter where
I may spend the night.

I glance across
my length of wing and
confirm the full good moon
in its proper station
off to the right,
lighting the trees below.

Lately I must keep
to the center of this
known world for this
orchard is pressed upon by
galaxies and cosmic dust.

Hush, enough - I spot a mouse.

SONG OF THE HUNT

Out through the ferns to a path that I know,
it edges the river above this high cliff.
Escape through the trees from the aim of his bow,
let his body grow tired, his muscles grow stiff.

Run, he is near,
no time for fear,
keep to the track,
don't look back.

My hooves slide on moss and tear the wet ground,
as long as I run he will have to run too, now
back to the woods through myrtle I pound, and
zigzag through nettle where Ram's-head once grew.

don't look back,
keep to the track,
no time for fear,
run, he is near.

The denser the forest the darker it gets,
the trees are now closer, the brambles so tight.
The rain turns the earth, slippery and wet,
in the heart of the woods I'll find safety at night.

No time for fear,
don't look back,
run, he is near,
keep to the track.

Where do I turn in the shadows to hide?
My hooves touch cold stone, I hear a bird's cry.
A sharp pain rips through me and tears me inside,
and here in this moment I know I will die.

I kept to the track,
and yet he is here.
I won't look back,
and I feel no fear.

Haiku for Story Time
Three Faerie Signs

Strands of broken pearls,
seeds scattered across the moss:
Queen of Fae was here.

The Hawthorn hedge pricks.
No mortal may climb this wall –
a dark Ælven curse.

Here by the far gate
beyond the last lantern light
a faerie portal.

Snow Queen Magic

Crystals,
crushed opals milky white,
banks of sparkling softness,
tints of blue a
quiet hue,
silent, frozen light.
Black branches
rising,
twisting,
stretching high
carry slippery
trickles of
silver
pearl-glazed ice,
building lacy bridges to
support the
misty sky.
Creaks and sudden
snapping cracks from
shaky marbled twigs,
a frosted chill,
burning sharp,
moonlit dark,
whirling, sweeping wind.
Sprinkled glitter,
speckled spray,
cold and filmy wet,
drifting lightly
downward from
empty distant heights,
adding to the smooth

deep hills that sleep with
restless sighs.
Droplets, melting
icy wood,
that catch again before
they fall,
the Snow Queen
makes a
a beauty trap –
holding still
her liquid will to
share with us this
winter's night.

THE FAERIE ENCOUNTER

"I'm not your friend," the faery firmly claimed
and scraped her thistle crown against my chin,
red droplets formed for which she took the blame;
she said to be my friend would be a sin.

"But still I leave you with a Faerie's Mark,
for times when you are feeling lost or low.
So here upon your chin I've etched a spark,
a star that in the dark will pulse and glow."

"Forever now you are in Faeries' debt.
Whether or not you use the Elven star,
I've bound you to our realm in time's deep net,
made from all there is both near and far."

With no more explanation she was gone.
The nighttime forest encircled me alone.
I wandered dazed until I reached the pond,
which meant somehow I'd finally made it home.

And now my life has never been the same,
for deer and even bear will walk with me,
and squirrels tease and act completely tame,
sharing nuts and drinking from my tea.

My friends and family treat me like I'm mad,
and ask me where I got my tattooed star.
They say the glow must come from something bad,
a poisonous dye that's made me odd and marred.

I spend my days and nights within the woods,
and forage what I need from what is there.
I know all herbs and mushrooms, which are good,
I've learned to balance all with love and care.

I live in two worlds now; belong to none,
and when I'm feeling sad, I touch the star -
sweet faerie songs then come and comfort some,
but the mark is both a blessèd-curse and scar.

And now until my days are truly done,
I have no choice but wait to really know,
by both great portals will I now be shunned?
To which dear realm will then I finally go?

ALIEN ANGELS

We are completely lost,
my husband, young daughter and I.
So we stop our car at a lone house
in a sunny cornfield on a bright autumn
day and climb the grey steps onto
the empty porch of a white
farmhouse with dark windows, and
ring the front doorbell.

Two children answer,
brother and sister.
The girl, maybe five,
assesses our presence with
eyes of cobalt-blue lightning,
the boy's emits solar-powered
violet sunsets.
Never have I seen
such eyes as these.
They hold at their center
old worlds from distant galaxies,
framed by perfect faces, too
perfect to be believed,
exquisite and ethereal.

The mother steps out of
interior shadows onto the porch –
a child now on either side.
They comprise a trilogy of angels.
But the mother's beauty
feels partly human, familiar.

Time stands still as
it always does in the
presence of cosmic fire.
We cannot speak –
what do you say when
you feel the urge to
bow your head and
avert your eyes?

"Your children are beautiful."
The mother smiles,
the autumn sun is
high and I feel peaceful.
All goes blank....and...
then... we're in the car driving,
on our way, the road familiar,
no longer lost.

THE HOUR WHEN THE VEIL IS THIN
A SEVEN-YEAR-OLD GIRL

There comes a sound.
It seems to rise up from
outside the far window,
down the dark hall,
facing this bedroom doorway,
where I sleep in the bed
that once had been my mom's.
I hear the sheer curtains flap in the night,
a summer storm is brewing and the window is open.
They left it open.
My skin breaks into goosebumps.
I'm wide awake,
frozen in the old bed,
weighted flat, the thin sheets
ripping as my feet stiffen with fear.

"Now I lay me down to sleep,"
The last words I'd said before
I'd closed my eyes.
But there, again, that sound:
A horror,
a wail,
woeful, but angry too…
malicious and surely not a dream.
Something wants in.
It wants this room and bed.
It wants me gone.

I can't scream, my vocal cords freeze,
my throat hurts like I've swallowed pure grief.
I'm choking with the need to call out and

something as ethereal as night shadows and
as heavy as lifetimes of deep regret,
slides up onto the blankets and
moves across the bed.

Then my father is yelling,
shaking me, telling me to wake up.
But my eyes are wide open.
Have been the whole time.
He calls to my mother,
but my mother doesn't come.

He puts a cold cloth on my face and neck.
I can breathe again.
He comforts me, questions me,
what has frightened me so? I am
drenched wet, feverish, shaking.
"Now I lay me down to sleep,"
only this escapes me.
He's angry now. "That damn prayer.
Why did she teach you that?
What a thing to tell a child."
I sit up slowly, my profound fear
disintegrating into exhaustion…
but still, I am afraid to be alone.
"I'll sleep here tonight,"
He reassures.
"You can sleep with Mommy."
He leaves the room.
I change into a fresh nightgown,
comb my damp and tangled hair.
Soon, we are trading places.
I slip into the now cool spot
that was my dad's, grateful.

"Mommy,
I was so frightened.
Something evil
came for me."
No response.
Instead, she turns
away from me and
curls into a ball.

It is raining.
I too turn, but toward the
open window,
this one views the lamppost,
the old oak, a piece of the street.
The sound of rain is sweet and
paired with the coming dawn,
it is both a cleaning and a
clearing of what is known,
what will be.

A fresh day arrives.
The sound of rain comforts.
First light enters the room
like an embrace.
I am still here.

COSMIC
TIME

COSMIC TOUR

When I die
I want the cosmic tour;
to break gravity,
pass GO
and swing out into the
stars, where
galaxies scatter like
so much salt on a
hearty meal.
I'll taste eternity,
sip from time and
feast till full.

The Dream Catcher's Song

At night the Dream Catcher comes for me,
an elegant latticework of pure energy,
a 3-D, multi-colored moving field or grid,
comprised of interlocking, vibrant pyramids.

It hovers above me, while I lie in my bed,
a sphere with a vortex swirling over my head.
Charges of light race around its clear tracks,
code upon code that no mortal can crack.

Is it calling me home with my own DNA?
Has my number been dialed or can I still stay?
Is it sending me elsewhere, a world dark and deep?
Will I wake here on earth or die in my sleep?

The Dream Catcher's here, what dreams does it take?
The Dream Catcher's here, what dreams does it make?

INDIGO BLACK

The top of the hill
darkens and makes
a sharp edge,
indigo-black,
across the landscape,
between earth and sky.
Here my eyes stop,
at this final place.
An aura pulsates at
this meeting point,
rising, falling.
My breath seems to
synchronize.
We are born,
breathe,
then grow
displaced and
hungry,
hungry, homesick,
helpless against the
sharp edge of
indigo black.

DOUBT

There are moments when my
smallness overwhelms me,
often as the sun's light hits the
edge of earth and morning dawns.

I turn quickly against the earth's axis,
retreating, spinning into a deep night,
an immense and all-consuming void,
spiraling with a rush of vertigo,
a punch to my core.

Here the words large and
small become meaningless.
I am aching at the center of myself,
slipping over the rim of
forever and
forgotten.

My breathing is not breath
but a contraction, expansion,
existing or extinguishing,
becoming,
unbecoming.

I am the Invisible
Shrinking Man, the
vastness of this last
awareness overwhelms
me, this brink at the
event horizon of
no return.

NIGHT LETTER

The wax kiss of the moon
pressed against the twilight sky
seals the edge
of day and night.

The last page is of dusk –
hieroglyphics of the now
folded up
into the past.

The mailbox of the night
opens up its sliding door
to reveal
the ancient sparks.

Eternity's familiar script,
forever the same message –
here is all
that is and was.

ODE TO A SUNSET

The sun drowns in Neptune's realm:
whose god then dies, yours or mine?
We've all tried to take life's helm,
while evening fades; transitions time.

With glimpses of a distant land,
Apollo bleeds across water.
We doubt we'll ever reach the sand -
Odysseus' lost sons and daughters.

The voyage back is eons long,
each of us a different song.
It's just a tale of getting home,
by painful choices, made alone.

TOMORROW'S MOUNTAIN

I stand on the edge of tomorrow's mountain
surrounded by all the time in the world,
my earthy wants have dimmed their shouting,
as life, a patterned rug, is now unfurled.
The land expands in every known direction,
in every way that space and time can grow.
Dancing algorithms and sparked connections
produce a single flash in which I'll know.

Here at last I stand in grace and wonder –
So much I thought was true all torn asunder.

Haiku - Cosmic

This is a dark night.
No moon to tell her tale,
only a false light.

Put thyme in your tea,
permeate your thoughts with sage,
sail the cosmic sea.

Inhale your last breath,
you are here among the stars,
exhale and release.

Six Transition Haiku
Read As a Single Poem

The night frogs' shrill chirps
mechanical like sad toys
left on in the dirt.

Fire flies snap on
like wooden matches struck once
then lost in the void.

Cold stars prick the sky,
pierce the night with pins of light,
teach mortality.

The night breeze turns cold.
I shiver at the woods edge,
step into the dark.

The frogs grow quiet.
It is neither night nor dawn
but where the veil thins.

I am rearranged.
My light has left my body,
an arrow sent home.

GOLDEN VARNISH

There are rich moments
when the sun bathes
me with its golden
varnish and I must
stop in my tracks and
receive its brush –
a full kinetic rush.

There are bright evenings
when the moon's kiss
transmits magic -
an electric charge
bringing visions of
yet to be joys,
and catastrophes.

There are dreams so real
waking seems the dream -
two lives are lived
simultaneously,
maybe many more,
where space and time
are the magic rhyme.

STAY WITH ME
FOR FRED

Stay with me. There is a little time left.
It is dusk and the meal is cleared away.
Buildings transform into smoky shapes,
an angled world of mauve and deeper blues.

This moment is layered like a poem,
lifetimes condensed into a slender space.
We have packed so much into these stanzas
with shared regrets as well as so much grace.

The sunset flames between the skyscrapers -
a fruit punch sky of orange and tangerine.
Above the night arrives with bright Venus
born whole and full on the Cosmos Sea.

This will be a night to remember.
When we say goodbye, meteors will fall.
I will recognize your voice eons in the future,
whatever voyages we are destined for.

IN ALL DIRECTIONS

I look out into a clear night's sky,
near the lake's edge and witness
constellations, bending space
in all directions, mapping,
designing, redefining my thoughts.
My mind, a finite book, is a small
world of questions, longing for larger
projects, other worlds and plans.

How easy it is to slide into a larger
object, one that seems grander,
with more purpose and weight.
But truly, when I do take the Big Slide,
might I find that the greatest treasures
are a cricket on the hearth, an autumn
leaf hanging on a twig, the pattern on
a moth's wings?

These projects, too, took eons to create.
What of the buzz of a bee, Beethoven's
5th and the cry of my newborn son –
the smell of warm milk or sweet ripened
strawberries, Mock Orange on a summer
evening, firefly blinks, the whack of a ball
hitting the bat, that just right kiss, as though
finally waking from a lonely dream.

So then, miracles are everywhere, we all
agree. But I haven't mentioned pain or loss....
the dark matter. This earth is surely heaven and
hell. The constellations bend me towards them,
stirring in me an objective-urge to
plunge and fly into the unknown.

What will I miss? So much.
What will I find?

As I stare into the lake's reflection,
I see a parallel sky, but the constellations
here are liquid and penetrable.
Right now, I could slip and fall through
time, into heaven or hell. I could
disappear and reappear in this *other*
place, one that differs but complements
our own...maybe not so different after all.

TELL ME WHO YOU ARE
FOR MY FATHER, LEON LAZARUS

Tell me who you are.
You've been tap, tapping, like Poe's Raven for
many a day in my mind and won't go away.

I look into the crackling fire and watch the flames
burst, like solar flares, but the light reveals nothing.

At night, asleep, but watchful in my dreams, I see
symbols, leaves swirling in a vortex, a rippling mirror,
the ebb and flow of tides in a star reflecting lake,
pulling like a magnet.

I catch a phrase, whispered but incoherent. Is that you?
One of my dead? My list grows ever longer.

The space of my life quickly bends and folds and here
I am, sliding straight to the edge of time; weighted by
the grand presence of matter,
toppling toward weightlessness,
so I can I finally break away.
But not quite yet.

I remember that last look, after your last exhalation, when you sat straight up in bed with fear and wonder in your eyes, seeing and hearing some new reality. Is that you then, sending Morse code out into the stars toward an old and distant home?

But everywhere is right here in an instant and there is no distance. You are here. You will be here when the time comes. So then, is it you tapping, or me tapping out to you?

GRANDPA LAZARUS AND THE LIGHT

You loved music. Oh, how I
wish I could have given you more,
your radio tinny and poor at the end.
Then I took my first flute lessons,
fourteen and proud to master a simple tune,
The Blue Tango, a song I knew you liked.
We sat alone, you in your chair
by the window, me on the
old couch, facing you.

Grandma had gone to the grocery store,
the apartment door clicked shut, and I
offered you my small accomplishment.
You looked so tired, and quiet and a
bit melancholy, but always a smile for me.
So, I clicked my flute together and began.

Your eyes closed and the simple tune rose.
It was then the light appeared:
a portal of blazing brilliance in front of you.
I could hardly bear its intensity.
Transfixed, my fingers still
played the keys,
a voice clear, male and resonant
spoke to me:

'Do not look into this light.
It is not meant for you.
This is the last time you will see
your grandfather alive,
but do not fear for him.
He will die holy.'

My fingers flew and such
heavenly music poured into the room,
trills, crescendos and diminuendos like
the first flutist at the philharmonic,
but the music was so unearthly, divine.
This could not be me playing?
Was I possessed by another's
transcended genius?

There my grandpa sat
still as death in his chair.
From his body an aura lifted,
a bluish white halo around his
entire being. The music
went on, magnificent, enthralling,
well beyond the borders of
this known world.

Then, like a door abruptly shut,
the light was gone and my hands,
with flute, fell heavy to my lap;
grandpa's aura snapped
back inside his mortal form.

I thought he was dead.
The words prophesized come to be.
But there was a flutter of his lids.
His gentle blue eyes opened,
a wisp of a smile appeared on his lips.

'Sherry, Sherry,
how did you play all that music?
I've never heard such music.
It was the most beautiful music in the world,
not of this world.
Everyone was there to greet me,
my mother, father, brothers and even
all my childhood friends.
And that music.
I wanted to leave right then,
but the music brought me back.'

That visit was our last time.
We spent a quiet afternoon,
Grandma back and cooking dinner,
but didn't share with her
the truth we'd just been shown.
The next day my father
came and brought me home.

He died the following week
and I felt my first deep grief.
I played the flute every day
for months, dreaming of
that celestial tune.

WHAT IS POSSIBLE?

I long to travel though the cosmos,
evolve, play with space and time,
create with pure consciousness.
I sense we are much more than what
we think we are, but fall so short in
this one small life.

I believe we can be magnificent,
we can be breathtaking,
play music like an angel,
if we dare.

To Pay the Crossing

Behind this cosmic screen there dwells a brilliant light,
that holds within pure energy, a massive force of might.

Its prescience is surging like a molten liquid sea,
so bright it is, there is no ray, can possibly go free.

A code's been made for everything; it reveals the needed break.
A key for every one of us; our means of sure escape.

As DNA has built and grown the tissues of our heart,
so too holds spirit, written truths, that let it come and part.

From here to there, pure consciousness is synonymous with time.
I plan to pay the crossing with a meter and a rhyme.

Acknowledgements

I want to start by thanking Barbara Lennox and Steve Griffin for their kind yet instrumental editorial input. *Falling through Time* has been improved and enriched by their thoughtful criticisms, notations and suggestions.

Barbara Lennox is a master poet and writer. I knew I would get an honest and constructive reading from her. Her insights were clear and her criticisms were thoughtful and well explained. Sometimes there was humor, often dry and delightful. I used the word "squish" and she pointed out to me it was quite a childish word in Scotland and the UK. I changed the word. I have a lot of readers from the United Kingdom. But I kept the word "sneakers" instead of "trainers" as no one says trainers in the US. Barbara gave each poem careful attention. The poems are better organized and more clearly understood because of her efforts. She also pointed out places where I went on too long and those poems are stronger by cutting back. I am proud to call her a colleague and a friend.

www.barbaralennox.com

@barbaralennoxwriter

Poetry: *The Ghost in the Machine*

Short story collection: *The Man Who Loved Landscapes*

Novels: *The Wolf in Winter* released November 2021 is the first book in her Trystan Trilogy, a telling of the ancient legend of Tristan and Isolde.

Steve Griffin, a master poet, with two wonderful books of poetry, as well as a very seasoned and superb author with many books to his name, has been an inspiration and has supported this project with enthusiasm. Steve's humor is exuberant and I so enjoyed that playfulness throughout his critiques. Steve is English and teased me about the amount of exclamation marks I used. There were way too many! I hadn't even realized it. I needed to show a bit more restraint. He helped make many a poem stronger by encouraging that restraint; showing me when enough, was enough. This always made the poem stronger. In one major poem, as he suggested, I removed the whole stanza. The poem was immediately stronger. But he then suggested that the stanza I removed might be made into another poem. That is what I wound up doing and it added to the thematic build up at the end of the book. I admire Steve's work a great deal and enjoyed working with him. I'm also proud to call him a friend and colleague.

www.steve-griffin.com

@stevegriffin.author

Books of poetry:

The Things We Thought Were Beautiful

Up in the Air

Novels: The Ghosts of Alice series, *The Boy in the Burgundy Hood* and *The Girl in the Ivory Dress*

The Secret of the Tirthas YA series

I am also deeply grateful to the many readers who read my book in advance of publication: Gail Engelbrecht, Angelica Takacs, Ellen Takacs, Gabriella Gonzalez Dellosso, Thandi Puren, Capella Riley, Diana Levenstein, Juliette Aristides, Ruth Miranda, Miryam Ginsburg and Janet Olson. All took the time and care to do so.

Capella Riley and I became friends on Instagram and have discovered we are kindred spirits. Thank you for your love and confidence in me. Capella read my children's novel, *The Vinetrope Adventures*, and fell in love with the world of vinetropes and then my poetry. I fell in love with her creativity, wisdom and emotional generosity, her knowledge of crystals and earth healing is amazing. She is currently writing her first book. @capella.deva

I would like to include Sebastian Engelbrecht, a master poet, writer and artist, for his support and words of encouragement over the last couple years. His wife, Gail Engelbrecht, who had read my other two books, then wonderfully volunteered to read this book as well and to share her insights. She found those last typos which cleaned and put the final "golden varnish" on the final edit. Thank you both so much. You have enriched my life. Sebastien is the author of DreamBook - Jaddamiah Jabberwocky (and the Things that Happen to People with Such Names), works of poetry and his fine art hangs on walls around the world.

www.sebastian-draconianletters.com @between.the.wordsandelsewhere and @draconianletters

Miryam Ginsburg and her husband Max go way back with me and my husband Fred and we have recently rekindled that acquaintance into true friendship. Max is one of our greatest artists, a master and much-loved teacher. Miryam is a wonderful sculptress. You jumped right on board to read an advanced copy of my book, Miryam, and I am truly grateful. We are so happy to have each other in our lives. I consider myself very fortunate to know you Miryam, and Max and your whole family and to be part of each other's support system.

@ginsburg.max www.maxginsburg.com

I met Ruth Miranda on Instagram and have read many of her beautiful books, becoming a fan. She is a superb writer and weaver of tales with high emotion. She read my children's novel and poetry. She has been very responsive to my poems and I was delighted when she offered to read my book in advance of publication. We are a great support system for each other. Some of her novels are: *Danseur, Alchemy of Chaos, The Heir of Avalon series: book 1 Avalon Hall, Book 2, A Darkening Fate, Book 3, Kingdom Come,* (newly released and completing the trilogy),*The Preternatural* series, *The Blood Trilogy* series.

@ruth_miranda

Jannet Olson is part of my writer's community on Instagram. She is a generous supporter of indie writers and gives of herself to that end. She generously offered to be part of my ARC readers and read my book in advance of publication. She has two wonderful books in her much loved *New Beginnings* series with a third to be released soon. Thank you, Janet, for your help and enthusiasm.

@janetolsonauthor

Diana Levenstein and I go way back to when our daughters were in nursery school together. Her humor and encouragement on all fronts has been invaluable for the last 35 years. Her empathy and compassion have helped me through many a trial. Her insights are invaluable. She has always been there for me and I hope she knows that I am there for her. I only have to think of her to feel better about anything.

Juliette Aristides has been a friend for over twenty years. She is one of our master artists, a master teacher, a best-selling author and founder and Director Emeritus of Aristides Atelier. She teaches workshops internationally. She has written six highly successful books on teaching the art of drawing and painting, which have been translated into six languages. *Still Life & Interior*, was recently released in 2021. Juliette refers to the visual art of drawing and painting as "The Poetics of Seeing." Poetry plays a role in her inspirations and as a teaching tool. It was a great joy for me to share my book with her in advance and pick up on our life long conversation on art, culture and poetry. Thank you so much Juliette. You are dear to me. www.aristidesarts.com
@juliettearistides

Gabriella Gonzalez Dellosso, is also a master artist and master teacher who is well known for her Narrative Realism and her "Poetic Portraits" in which poetry often plays an important role for inspiration. She is also a writer who writes on art and poetic expression. She is recognized for her homage to historical women in paintings, using self-portraits that place her into the poetic vision of these great women. Her maternal grandmother and great-grandfather were respected and published poets in their lifetimes in South America. Her grandmother, Carmen Galvez de Jalil was a cultural force like her granddaughter. Our friendship goes back over twenty years and we reconnected recently. She offered her support to read this book in advance and I am honored that she has done so. Thank you, Gabriela.
www.gabrieladellossoart.com
@gabrielagonzalezdellosso

Angelica Takacs and her mom, Ellen Takacs, are artists and make hand-crafted jewelry. I fell in love with their jewelry and have a collection of their original pieces, some with hand painted scenes. They both read my 1st book of poems, *Seeds of the Pomegranate*. Ellen said she cried when she read some of them; that they touched her heart. She also is a poet. They have been steadfast supporters, wonderful people and true creatives. Thank you, Angelica and Ellen. I'm so glad I discovered you both.
@the_goblinfaire

Thandi Puren, a British actress, most recently in the role of Trish in *Ernie Barbarash's Holiday in the Wild*, and Ruby in *The Lullaby* (2017) was introduced to me by Capella, and offered to read the manuscript and support this project. Poems must also sound well when read out loud and often are more powerful when you do so. So, I thought it would be great to have a professional actress read my poems. Thank you Thandi, for your time. @thandipuren

Another big and heartfelt thanks goes to Becky and James Wright at Platform House Publishing for bringing this baby to life and into the world. Thank you, Becky, for the beautiful internal design and formatting and James for the spectacular cover. You worked with me every step of the way, made me feel part of the process and always did so with patience and kindness. The book is beautiful thanks to both of you. And as you know, Becky, I am a huge fan of your books and your dark and beautiful writing.
www.beckywrightauthor.com
@beckywrightauthor
@platformhousepublishing
www.platformhousepublishing.com

To Julie Bell, my friend forever, you have boosted my spirits and raised my confidence so many times, I can't even count. You honored me by illustrating my children's fantasy novel and made it a most beautiful book, bringing my characters to life. You are one of the great fine artists out there in the world, bringing beauty and meaning to culture and delighting and uplifting those who see your amazing works. Your energy, optimism and enthusiasm are contagious. Our conversations on endless subjects always leaves me excited about life, even in dark times. When I doubt my own creative potential, you bounce me right back into the pulse of things. Thank you.
www.juliebell.com
@juliebellartist

An extra huge hug and thank you goes to Dr. Vern G. Swanson. Vern has been the dearest of friends for forty years. He and his whole family, which now consists of five grandchildren, are lifelong friends with our whole

family and two grandchildren. We have shared a love of culture, art and spiritual inquiry throughout our friendship. Vern is a world-renowned art historian, author and lecturer and former Director of the Springville Museum of Art in Utah for 35 years. I am so honored he wrote the Foreward to this book. I'm completely overwhelmed by his in-depth reading and then his beautiful words about the book. Outside of my immediate family, no one has supported me more.
www.verngswanson.wordpress.com

My dear sister, Rochelle Lazarus Saxena, alpha and beta read this book. Yes, this was maybe not as an objective a reading as from a colleague, but my sister is by profession a writer and editor for over thirty years and I knew she would bring both her professionalism and her personal and intimate understanding of my work into her reading. She read through the manuscript several times, as well as seeing many of the poems in advance over the last couple years. She made many insightful suggestions. A change in a single word makes a great difference in a poem and she naturally and automatically looked for typos, misspellings and errors in grammar. Her emotional support was uplifting and encouraging throughout the project and she always lent me her ear when it was needed. All my love to you my dear sister. We are there for each other always.

To my daughter, Kara L. Ross, thank you from the bottom of my heart. You have been listening to my poetry since you were a child and you are a wonderful writer, art historian, scholar, curator and poet yourself. You are a mother now too, with a demanding career and you remain the most wonderful of daughters. You have the ability to read, then analyze and go right to the core of something that isn't quite working and figure it out. You also have a gift for order and organizing and can quickly tell what poems belong where and how to order them, helping me on several occasions, especially with my haiku arrangements. Thank you for your insights and your love. I love you fiercely and I am so proud of you.
www.artrenewal.org

Kara Lysandra Ross has published articles in *Fine Art Connoisseur Magazine* and the *Epoch Times* and is the COO and Co-Chairperson for The Art Renewal Center, a non-profit art educational foundation. She also curates all their traveling exhibitions. She is writing the Catalog Raisonne on the British 19th Century artist, Edmond Blair Leighton, wrote a chapter in the second edition of *The Life and Works of William Bouguereau, published by* ACC Art Books and co-wrote the book *William Bouguereau, The Essential Works*, published by ACC Art Books.

And last here in my acknowledgements, but always the first in my heart, I thank you, my dear husband of 52 years, Fred Ross, for sharing your life with me. We are eternal kindred spirits, best friends and never seem to tire of talking to each other. We can also remain silently comfortable, working side by side. You always loved my poetry, from when we first met, when I was only eighteen. My one poem in this volume, "The Snow Queen," is actually a poem I wrote when I was sixteen. It is the only poem from my youth, and I did edit it some for this book, but it remains mostly as it was. You read it that summer that we met and were so taken with it, you said you knew then you loved me. You have been the biggest supporter of my poetry, writing and of me, giving me a deep sense of comfort, of belonging and of being at home in your presence. You are my biggest fan, and I hope you know I am yours. I love you now and forever.

Fred Ross Founder and Co-Chairperson of The Art Renewal Center, university and museum lecturer, articles for *The Epoch Times*, Co-author and patron of *The Life and Works of William Bouguereau*, Published by ACC Art Books, Co-author of the book *William Bouguereau, The Essential Works, published by* ACC Art Books.
www.artrenewal.org

Photo by Kara Ross

Sherry Ross was editor-in-chief of The Art Renewal Center, (www.artrenewal.org) known as ARC, for 15 years and still offers her editorial services. ARC is a non-profit art educational foundation and website, offering yearly art scholarships and sponsoring the famous International ARC Salon Competition, the largest competition in the world for Contemporary Realism, with a traveling exhibition of winners and finalists, held in NYC (at Sotheby's New York in 2021) and at the MEAM Museum (Museum of Modern European Art) in Barcelona, Spain. She has also written articles on art for the ARC website.

Falling Through Time is Ross's second collection of poems. Ms. Ross' first collection, *Seeds of the Pomegranate*, 2000, was inspired by the Persephone myth, and its themes touch on loss and rebirth in a contemporary world through observation and engagement in nature. The core of this collection, a chapbook, was a runner up for publication in a national contest sponsored by <u>POET</u> magazine.

Sherry L. Ross studied with the poet David Ignatow for three semesters at the 92nd St. Y, (YM-YWHA) in Manhattan, in the early 80s. Ignatow is remembered for his seminal works on the common person, finding wisdom in everyday life. Ms. Ross credits Ignatow with giving her clarity of vision in her poems. "He taught me focus, that each poem must hold a core theme: a purpose." Ross also studied with Marguerite Young (Miss Macintosh My Darling) at Seton Hall University in the 70s.

Ross is also author of a children's fantasy novel for eight-year-olds + up: *The Vinetrope Adventures*, Book One, *Return of the Vinetropes*, illustrated by Julie Bell. www.juliebell.com

The Vinetrope Adventures' website can be found at www.vinetrope.com or check out Ms. Ross's fanciful Instagram account @thevinetropeadventures for glimpses into her garden, excerpts and poems, book reviews and fantasy photo shoots. Book two of *The Vinetrope Adventures* is due out in late 2022 and is entitled, *A Dangerous World*. Ross will be including some of her own drawings in the second book. She studied at The Art Students League in NYC in her twenties and continues to draw for pleasure.

She is also author of a cookbook, many years ago entitled: The Sorrell Ridge Cookbook.

Sherry collects miniatures for her faerie village, (indoors and out) as well as antique and contemporary toys and dolls and creates photo shoots with her collections.

Ms. Ross now resides in a house in the woods, surrounded by nature and she loves to garden. She lives with her husband of fifty-two years and Sammy the Cat, and happily, also, near her daughter Kara son-in-law, Sean, and two granddaughters, Kayleigh and Anna. She is always on the lookout for natural phenomena and sprites and faeries as she walks the woods just one step out the gate in her backyard.